ILLUSTRATIONS

OF VARIOUS STYLES OF

INDIAN ARCHITECTURE

A SERIES OF FIFTEEN PHOTOGRAPHS
OF SOME OF THE MOST IMPORTANT BUILDINGS IN INDIA
ERECTED BETWEEN B.C. 250 AND A.D. 1830,
WITH

A LECTURE ON THE STUDY OF INDIAN ARCHITECTURE

READ AT A MEETING OF THE SOCIETY OF ARTS,
ON 19TH DECEMBER, 1866

ILLUSTRATIONS

OF VARIOUS STYLES OF

INDIAN ARCHITECTURE

A SERIES OF FIFTEEN PHOTOGRAPHS
OF SOME OF THE MOST IMPORTANT BUILDINGS IN INDIA
ERECTED BETWEEN B.C. 250 AND A.D. 1830,

WITH

A LECTURE ON THE STUDY OF INDIAN ARCHITECTURE

READ AT A MEETING OF THE SOCIETY OF ARTS,
ON 19TH DECEMBER, 1866

By

JAMES FERGUSSON

GYAN

Published by

GYAN

Gyan Publishing House
5, Ansari Road
Daryaganj, New Delhi-110002
Phone: 011-47034999, 9811692060
E-mail: books@gyanbooks.com

Distribution Network
gyanbooks.com
India, USA, Canada, UK, Australia

ISBN: 978-93-6433-125-8 (PB)
First Published, 1869

2nd Impression 2024

Printed at: Gyan Press, Delhi.

ILLUSTRATIONS OF VARIOUS STYLES OF INDIAN ARCHITECTURE & ON THE STUDY OF INDIAN ARCHITECTURE

Author: JAMES FERGUSSON

SCIENCE AND ART DEPARTMENT
OF THE COMMITTEE OF COUNCIL ON EDUCATION,
SOUTH KENSINGTON MUSEUM.

ILLUSTRATIONS

OF VARIOUS STYLES OF

INDIAN ARCHITECTURE.

A SERIES OF FIFTEEN PHOTOGRAPHS
OF SOME OF THE MOST IMPORTANT BUILDINGS IN INDIA
ERECTED BETWEEN B.C. 250 AND A.D. 1830.

WITH

A LECTURE ON THE STUDY OF INDIAN ARCHITECTURE,

READ AT A MEETING OF THE SOCIETY OF ARTS, ON 19TH DECEMBER, 1866,

By JAMES FERGUSSON, F.R.S.

AND A REPORT OF THE DISCUSSION WHICH ENSUED.

LONDON:
PRINTED FOR THE USE OF SCHOOLS OF ART
IN THE UNITED KINGDOM.
1869.

PREFACE.

The photographs which are included in this little volume were selected with a view of showing the beauty of decoration, and the immense variety of style, which are to be met with in the great buildings which still exist among the cities and plains of India.

The study of Indian architecture ought, for many reasons, to be most interesting to all Englishmen: and now that photographers have sent over to this country sun-pictures of hundreds of the chief monuments of the Buddhist, Hindú, and Mahommedan religions, the student is offered every opportunity of tracing the history and progress of an art which had a splendid existence of upwards of sixteen centuries.

The subject of Indian Architecture has been treated at some length by Mr. Fergusson in the last edition of his 'History of Architecture in all Countries,' and to this work, from which the following descriptions were (with permission) chiefly taken, the student is referred for further information.

In the Art Library at the South Kensington Museum there are many valuable illustrated works on Indian Architecture, including several volumes of photographs, which may at all times be consulted. And at present an exhibition of more than two hundred Indian photographs, collected and arranged by Mr. Fergusson, may be seen in an adjoining room.

J. C.

August, 1869.

CONTENTS.

*** *All the Plates, except No. 11, are produced by the Photo-relief Printing Company, and are absolutely permanent.*

THE SANCHI TOPE.

From a Photograph by Lieutenant Waterhouse, R.A.

THE SANCHI TOPE.

IN BHOPAL, CENTRAL INDIA.

BUDDHIST.*

Probable date of the Tope † . . . B.C. 500.
Ditto *Stone Railing*, B.C. 250.
Ditto *Gateways* . . A.D. 19 to 37.

THE TOPE‡ at Sanchi, near Bilsah, in Central India, is by far the finest, as well as the most perfect, in that country. The principal building consists of a dome 106 feet in diameter, and 42 feet in height.

The fence by which this Tope is surrounded is extremely curious. It consists of stone posts 8 feet 8 inches high, and little more than 2 feet apart, surmounted by a plain architrave, and between every two uprights three horizontal cross-pieces of stone are inserted.

Still more curious are the four gateways, one of which (the eastern) is shown in the photograph. It consists of two square pillars, covered with sculptures with bold elephant capitals, rising to a height of 18 feet 4 inches; above this are three lintels slightly curved upwards in the centre and ending in Ionic scrolls; they are supported by continuations of the

* *Gautama Buddha, the founder of this religion, died* 543 *years* B.C.

† *General Cunningham.*

‡ *A solid mound of masonry, sometimes dedicated to Buddha, or erected over the relics of Buddhist priests.*

columns, and three uprights inserted in the spaces between the lintels. They are covered with elaborate sculpture, and surmounted by emblems. The total height is 33 feet 6 inches.

One gateway, the northern, has fallen, and if removed to this country would raise the character of Indian sculpture, as nothing comparable to it has yet been transported from that part of the world to Europe.—*Fergusson.*

Temple of Marttand.—View Looking East.

From a Photograph by Mr. Burke.

KASHMIR.

TEMPLE OF MARTTAND, OR THE SUN.

VIEW LOOKING EAST.

Probable, date A.D. 490–555.

Of all the existing remains of Kashmirian grandeur the most striking in size and situation is the noble ruin of Marttand. The mass of building now known by the name of Matan, or Marttand, consists of one lofty central edifice with a small detached temple on each side of the entrance, the whole standing in a large quadrangle surrounded by a colonnade of fluted pillars, with intervening trefoiled headed recesses.

The exterior measurement of the central building is 61 feet long by 41 feet wide. The whole interior and exterior surfaces are ornamented with rich sculptures, which have been defaced and destroyed by the hand of the Mahommedan. 'The Temple,' says General Cunningham, 'was dedicated to the Sun, who was "Brahma," or Creator at morn; "Vishnu," or the Preserver at noon; and "Siva," or the Destroyer at even.'—*Lieut. H. H. Cole, R.E.*

Temple of Marttand.—View of Peristyle.

From a Photograph by Mr. Burke.

KASHMIR.

TEMPLE OF MARTTAND, OR THE SUN.

VIEW OF PERISTYLE, NORTH SIDE OF ENCLOSURE.

Probable date, A.D. 693 *to* 729.

THE Temple of Marttand is enclosed by a pillared quadrangle, 244 feet in length by 168 feet in breadth, containing 84 fluted columns. This number was probably fixed with design, being the famous 'chourási' (84) of the Hindús, and is specially emblematic of the 'Sun.' Thus even the Colonnade is made typical of the Deity to whom the Temple is consecrated.—

Lieut. H. H. Cole, R.E.

THE KYLAS AT ELLORA. (*Ninth or Tenth Century.*)

From a Photograph.

THE KYLAS AT ELLORA.

HINDÚ—*Ninth or Tenth Century.*

ONE of the most interesting ornaments of Hindú architecture is the rock-cut temple at Ellora,* generally known as the Kylas (*Paradise*). Its beauty and singularity have always excited the astonishment of travellers, and in consequence it is better known than almost any other structure in that country, from the numerous views and sketches of it that have been published. It is not a mere interior chamber cut in the rock, but is a model of a complete temple such as might have been erected on the plain. In other words, the rock has been cut away externally as well as internally.

No insular rock being available, a pit was dug in the sloping side of a hill, about 270 feet in length and 150 feet wide. In the centre of this rectangular court stands the temple, consisting of a vimana between 80 feet and 90 feet in height, preceded by a large square porch supported by sixteen columns; before this stands a detached porch (*shown in the photograph*) reached by a bridge; and in front of all stands the gateway, which is in like manner connected

* *Ellora is about 200 miles north-east of Bombay.*

COLONNADE OF HINDÚ PILLARS. (*Eleventh Century.*)
From a Photograph by Mr. Bourne.

COLONNADE OF HINDÚ PILLARS,

NEAR THE KOOTUB AT DELHI.

HINDÚ — *Eleventh Century.*

At the end of the twelfth century the Great Ghorian conqueror, Shahab ud-deen, entered India and defeated Pirthay, the Rajah of Delhi. This success was followed by the conquest of Canouge; and after the fall of these two cities—the capitals of the greatest Empires in the Peninsula—India may be said to have been conquered.

At the death of Shahab in 1206, his great Empire fell to pieces, and India fell to the share of one of his greatest Generals, Kootub ud-deen Ibek.

In order to perpetuate the memory of his conquest of the Hindús, Kootub erected a tall column of victory (the Kootub Minar) within the precincts of the Palace of the unfortunate Rajah Pirthay, and around this column a group of ruins of the old palace still remains. Even in situation these ruins are singularly beautiful, for they stand on the gentle slope of a hill, over-looking a plain that had once apparently been a lake, but which afterwards became the site of three successive Capitals of the East.

COLONNADE OF HINDÚ PILLARS.

It is a little difficult to determine whether the pillars now stand as originally arranged by the Hindús, or whether they have been taken down and re-arranged by the conquerors. They are of the same order as those used at the Jaina Temple on Mount Abu, except that those at Delhi are much richer and more elaborate. They belong probably to the eleventh or twelfth century, and are among the few specimens to be found in India that seem to be over-loaded with ornament, there not being one inch of plain surface from the capital to the base. Still the ornament is so sharp and so cleverly executed, and the effect in their present state of decay and ruin so picturesque, that it is very difficult to find fault with what is so beautiful.—*Fergusson.*

TEMPLE OF SIVA, HULLABEED. *Thirteenth Century.*

From a Photograph by Dr. Neill.

TEMPLE OF SIVA AT HULLABEED.

SCULPTURED DECORATIONS OF THE SOUTH-WEST FRONT OF THE SOUTHERN VIMANA.

HINDÚ — *Thirteenth Century.*

THE great Temple of Hullabeed* was unfortunately never finished, the works having been stopped by the Mahommedan conquest in 1310, after they had been in progress apparently for eighty-six years. This building is 160 ft. north and south by 122 ft. east and west. The height, as it now remains, to the cornice, is about 25 ft. from the terrace on which it stands.

The material out of which the Temple is erected is an indurated pot-stone of volcanic origin, found in the neighbourhood. This stone is said to be soft when first quarried, and easily cut in that state, though hardening on exposure to the atmosphere; its enduring qualities seem to be unrivalled, for though neglected and exposed to all the vicissitudes of a tropical climate for more than six centuries, the minutest details are as clear and sharp as on the day they were finished.

* *On the eastern coast of South India.*

TEMPLE OF SIVA AT HULLABEED.

The building stands on a terrace about five feet high, and paved with large slabs. On this stands a frieze of Elephants, following all the sinuosities of the ground-plan, and extending to some 710 ft. in length, and containing not less than two thousand elephants, sculptured as only an Oriental can represent the wisest of brutes. Above these is a frieze of conventional lions; then comes a scroll of infinite beauty and variety of design; over this is a frieze of horsemen and another scroll; over which is a bas-relief of scenes from the Ramayana, representing the conquest of Ceylon and all the varied incidents of that epic. Then come celestial beasts and celestial birds, and all along the east front a frieze of groups from human life, and then a cornice, with a rail, divided into panels, each containing two figures. Over this are windows of pierced slabs. In the centre, in place of the windows, is first a scroll and then a frieze of gods and heavenly apsaras, dancing girls, and other objects of Hindú mythology. This frieze, which is about 5 ft. 6 in. in height, is continued all round the western front of the building, and extends to some 400 ft. in length. Siva, with his consort Parvati seated on his knee, is repeated at least fourteen times; Vishnu in his nine Avatars even oftener. Brahma occurs three or four times, and every great god of the Hindú Pantheon finds his place. Some of these are carved with a minute elaboration of detail which can only be reproduced by photography, and may probably be considered as the most marvellous exhibition of patient human labour that the world ever produced.—*Fergusson.*

PORCH AT BEEJANUGGER. *(Sixteenth Century.)*

From a Photograph by Dr. Neill.

PORCH OF THE TEMPLE OF VITOBA AT BEEJANUGGER.

Hindú—*Sixteenth Century.*

At Beejanugger * there is a Porch erected in the 16th century. . . . As in almost every instance in the Dravidian temples of Southern India, the material employed is granite, each pier being generally one single stone, placed in position in a rough form, and the little shafts and ornaments afterwards detached by undercutting. It is difficult to realize the amount of labour bestowed on this porch, but we must award to the Dravidians the palm for patient industry over all the builders in the world.

Where subordination of parts is preserved, the general effect of these choultries and porches is pleasing, and from their vastness, sometimes almost reaches to sublimity.

* *In Southern India.*

MOHÁFIZ KHAN'S MOSQUE, AHMEDABAD. (*Sixteenth Century.*)

From a Photograph by Col. Biggs, R.A.

MOHÁFIZ KHAN'S MOSQUE, AHMEDABAD.

BASE OF THE SOUTHERN MINARET.

MAHOMMEDAN—*Sixteenth Century.*

THE details of this Mosque are exquisite, and it retains its minarets, which is too seldom the case. As will be seen from the photograph, the lower part of the minaret is of pure Hindú architecture; all the bases at Ahmedabad are neither more nor less than the perpendicular parts of the basement of Hindú or Jaina temples elongated. . . . On the angles of all Hindú temples are niches containing images; this the Moslems could not tolerate, so they filled them with tracery. After a century's experience they produced forms which, as architectural ornaments, will in their own class, stand comparison with any employed in any age, or in any part of the world; and in doing this, they invented a class of window-tracery in which they are also unrivalled.

Above the roof of the Mosques the minarets are always round towers slightly tapering, as in the Mosque of Moháfiz Khan, relieved by galleries displaying great richness in the brackets which support them, as well as in the balustrades which serve for protection. The tower always terminates in a conical top, relieved by various disks. They are, so far as I know, the only minarets which surpass those of Cairo in beauty of outline or richness of detail, excepting those of the Ranee Seepree Mosque, which are still more beautiful.—*Fergusson.*

PALACE OF THE SULTANA.—FUTTEHPORE SIKRI. (*Sixteenth Century.*)

From a Photograph by Mr. Bourne.

PALACE OF THE SULTANA—FUTTEHPORE SIKRI,

NEAR AGRA.

MAHOMMEDAN — *Sixteenth Century.*

FUTTEHPORE SIKRI, near Agra, was long the favourite residence of Akbar (A.D. 1556-1605), the greatest sovereign of his race, and he adorned it with a series of buildings as remarkable as anything of their class to be found in India. A strong feeling for Hindú art prevails throughout, and the whole is stamped with that bold originality which marked every act of the great man to whom they owe their origin.

The palace has no pretension to be regarded as one great architectural object; but as a picturesque group of elegant buildings, it is unrivalled. All are built of the red sandstone of the hill on which the palace stands; no marble is used and no stucco, either inside or out, all the ornaments being honestly carved in relief on the stone. The roofs as well as the floors are all of the same material, and characterised by that singular Hindú-like aversion to an arch which Akbar alone, of all the Moslem monarchs, seems to have adopted.—*Fergusson.*

TOMB OF ETMADDOWLA. *(Sixteenth Century.)*

From a Photograph by Mr. Bourne.

TOMB OF ETMADDOWLA,

NEAR AGRA.

MAHOMMEDAN—*Sixteenth Century.*

THE neighbourhood of Agra is crowded with the Tombs of Nobles of the Court, some of them scarcely less magnificent than those of their masters. Among these, one, erected by Etmaddowla, the Minister of Akbar, for himself, is one of the most splendid in elaboration, though far from being the most graceful in design. The whole is of white marble and inlaid with precious stones in various patterns, to a greater extent, perhaps, than any other building in India.—*Fergusson.*

THE TAJ MEHAL AT AGRA. (*Seventeenth Century.*)

From an Engraving

THE TAJ MEHAL AT AGRA.

Seventeenth Century.

THE Taj Mehal at Agra was erected by the Emperor Shah Jehan, about 1645, to contain the remains of his favourite wife. It was his intention to have erected his own tomb on the opposite side of the river Jumna, but this he did not carry into effect, and he was buried near his wife in the Taj. The building consists of a platform 18 feet high and about 300 feet square. On, and in the centre of this is the tomb, 186 feet square, with corners cut off to the extent of 33 feet 9 inches; the Dome is 58 feet in diameter and 80 feet in height. The whole structure is faced with white marble inlaid with precious stones, arranged in designs of exquisite beauty; and the judgment with which this style of ornament is applied to the features of the building gives a high idea of the skill and taste of the designer.—*Lieut. H. H. Cole, R.E.*

INTERIOR OF THE PALACE AT DELHI. (*Seventeenth Century.*)

From a Photograph by Mr. Bourne.

THE PALACE AT DELHI.

INTERIOR OF THE DEWANNEE KHAS.

MAHOMMEDAN—*Seventeenth Century.*

ON the accession of Shah Jehan (1628), the Mahommedan style again flourished in all its magnificence. It was this King who built the present city of Delhi, with its great Mosques and Palaces, the latter the most perfect and complete examples of the style in India.

The principal entrance to the Palace at Delhi faces the Chaudnee Chouk, a splendid wide street, nearly a mile long, planted with two rows of trees and with a canal of water flowing down its centre. Entering within the deeply-recessed portal, you find yourself beneath the roof of a vaulted hall, similar in plan to a Gothic cathedral, many of which it exceeds in dimensions. Opposite to this great entrance is the Dewannee Khas, or principal hall, containing in its centre directly facing the entrance a niche richly ornamented, where on a platform of marble, inlaid with precious stones, once stood the famous peacock throne. To the left of this great court is a smaller one, containing the private hall of audience. It is round the frieze of this hall that the famous inscription runs, 'If there is a heaven on earth it is this, it is this.'—*Fergusson.*

SUMÉREE TEMPLE AT RAMNUGGER. (*Eighteenth Century.*)

From a Photograph by Mr. Bourne.

SUMÉREE TEMPLE AT RAMNUGGER,

NEAR BENARES.

HINDÚ—*Eighteenth Century.*

BENARES is one of the most picturesque and beautiful cities in India, and may be one of the oldest. No building, however, exists in it now whose date is anterior to the thirteenth century; almost all those on the banks of the river, one of which is represented in the accompanying photograph, being of comparatively recent date.

Lower Part of Sumeree Temple at Ramnugger.

From a Photograph by Mr. Bourne.

SUMÉREE TEMPLE AT RAMNUGGER.

NEAR BENARES.

HINDÚ—*Eighteenth Century.*

SCULPTURE IN THE LOWER PORTION.

THE lower portion of the Temple at Ramnugger is divided into panels which are filled with various sculptured decorations, among which the elephant, as usual, figures prominently.

Many of the Gods of Hindú mythology are likewise represented with their usual accompaniments.

Sikh Temple at Amritsir.

From a Photograph.

SIKH TEMPLE AT AMRITSIR.

SIKH—*Nineteenth Century.*

THE Temple at Amritsir,* of which the photograph represents a view of the interior, owes its existence to the magnificence of the late Rajah, Runjeet Sing. It shows great splendour, but a marked decline in taste from the temples erected in India proper, either contemporaneously, or at an earlier date.—*Fergusson.*

* (*The Pool of Immortality*) *In the Punjaub—near Lahore.*

ON

THE STUDY

OF

INDIAN ARCHITECTURE.

READ AT A MEETING OF THE SOCIETY OF ARTS,

ON WEDNESDAY, 19TH DECEMBER, 1866.

BY JAMES FERGUSSON, F.R.S.

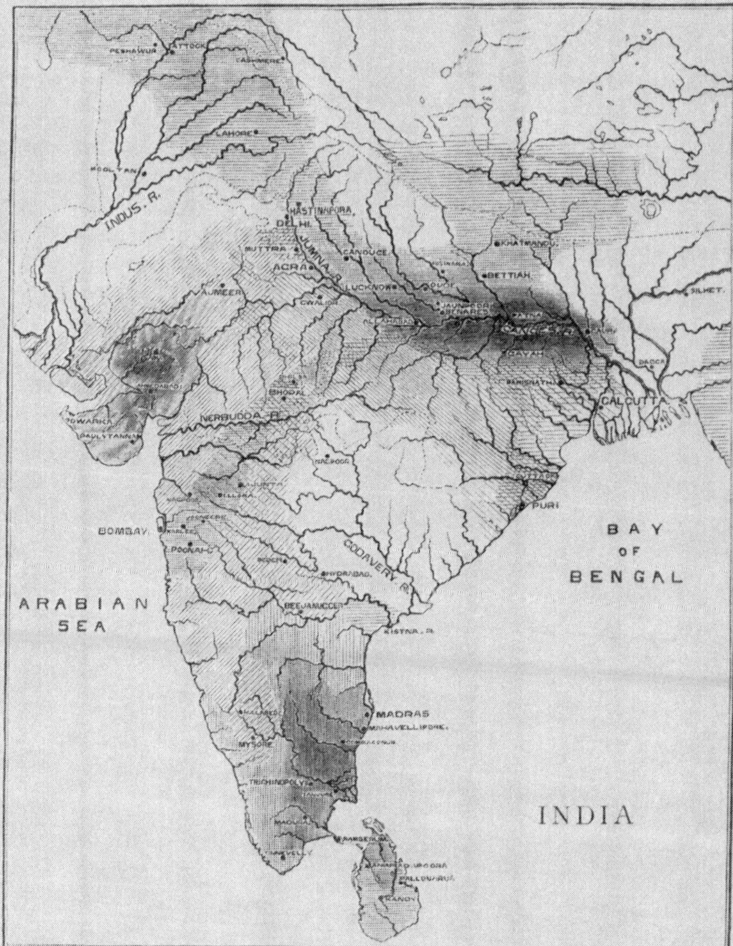

SKETCH MAP OF INDIA.

Showing the approximate Distribution of the four principal Styles of Hindu Architecture, viz. :—

Buddhist, distinguished by horizontal hatching ... ...

Dravidian, by perpendicular lines ... ...

Northern Hindu, by lines sloping to the right ... ...

Chalukya and Jaina, by lines sloping to the left ... ...

With the Sanction of the Science and Art Department of the Committee of Council on Education.

ON

THE STUDY

OF

INDIAN ARCHITECTURE

READ AT A MEETING OF THE SOCIETY OF ARTS

ON WEDNESDAY, 19TH DECEMBER, 1866,

BY JAMES FERGUSSON, F.R.S.

With a Report of the Discussion which ensued.

LONDON:
JOHN MURRAY, ALBEMARLE STREET.
1867.

ON THE

STUDY OF INDIAN ARCHITECTURE.

By JAMES FERGUSSON, F.R.S.

The varieties of the styles of Indian Architecture are so numerous, and their relations to one another so complex, that it would be impossible to convey even an elementary idea of the subject without entering into details and employing an amount of illustration which would be utterly incompatible with the extent of a single lecture. All, therefore, that I propose to attempt on the present occasion is, to try to explain to you the importance of the study of Indian Art. First, as bearing directly on our knowledge of India itself; secondly, as elucidating the true position of Architecture in this country;—in doing this, I will also endeavour to point out which are the principal means by which a knowledge of that art may be obtained.

When I was in India, between twenty and thirty years ago, the subject of Indian Architecture had hardly been touched. Views of Indian buildings had, it is true, been published by Daniell and others, but no attempt had been made to classify them, and the vaguest possible ideas prevailed as to their age or relative antiquity. At that time, thanks to the learning and enthusiasm of Mr. James Prinsep, great progress was being made in the decipherment of Indian inscriptions, and the study of the antiquities of the country, and I determined to try if the architecture could not be brought within the domain of science. For several years I pursued the study almost unremittingly, and bit by bit the mystery unravelled itself. I learnt that there was not only one Hindu, and one Mohamedan style in India, but several species of each class; that these occupied well-defined local provinces, and belonged each to ascertained ethnological divisions of the people. I also found out, much to my disappointment, that the boasted primæval antiquity of the rock-cut examples was a myth; and that the whole could be arranged into consecutive series, with well-defined boundaries.

The results of these investigations were published in various forms after my return from India. Like most previous works of their class, however, they were, from the nature of their illustrations, both cumbrous and expensive. This has hitherto had the effect of limiting the knowledge of Indian Architecture to the few who were rich enough to purchase such works, and no general interest in the subject is diffused among the public at large. These difficulties were probably inherent in the nature of the subject, and it is not very easy to see how the requisite information could have been rendered accessible, had it not been that Photography has latterly been extensively employed in the illustration of Indian Art, and several splendid photographic works been published on the subject. And owing to the subscriptions of several natives of Bombay, and the gratuitous co-operation of others, these have been given to the public at prices below the cost of production. In addition to these, new sets of Photographs are constantly being sent home from India. Almost all the best-known buildings have been taken—some very imperfectly, it must be confessed, but still sufficiently well to authenticate or correct previous illustrations, and any one, at a small expense, may now make himself master of any branch of the inquiry. For myself I may say, that I have learnt as much, if not more, of Indian Architecture during the last two or three years, than I did during my residence in India, and I now see that the whole subject may be made intelligible, and I see how it can be done. The defect of what has been undertaken hitherto is, that it has been done without system, and that unless the investigator has such previous knowledge as I happened to obtain when in the East, it is difficult to know where to begin; and this difficulty will, I fear, remain till some good handbook or grammar of the subject is published. I have attempted something of the sort in the volume of my history just published, but it is meagre and far too short. 300 pages and 200 woodcuts will not suffice for so vast a subject, and something more must be done before the study of Indian Architecture will be easy or popular.

As hinted above, the interest of the study of Indian Art is twofold, the most legitimate branch being that which directly concerns India itself, and which, consequently, we will take first.

It is of course difficult for me to guess what information my present audience may have on this subject, but this I know, that, in general society, very few have clear ideas of who the inhabitants of India are, or whence they came. With most people the Hindus, or as they used to be called, the Gentoos, are one people, at least as uniform as the Germans or French, and worshipping certain gods, whom they have superstitiously reverenced from time immemorial. When you begin to look below the surface you find the case is widely different. In the first place, the valley of the Ganges was, at the very dawn of history, inhabited by races whom we now are forced to call aboriginal, as we know nothing of their origin, and we find detached fragments of them existing in the hills under the name of Bhils, Coles, Gonds, &c. Leaving them for a moment, we find there a people whom we call Aryans, who came into India across the Upper Indus, it may be about 2000 years before Christ, or even earlier. They first settled in the Punjaub; then on the water-shed between the Sutlej and the Jumna; and, lastly, in Oude and further eastward. These were the Sanscrit-speaking races, to whom we owe all the important literary productions of India.

After a thousand years' sojourn in India they lost their purity of race, apparently by intermingling with the aboriginal races, and by the innate decay of enervation by the climate.

This enabled a prophet called Sakya Muni, or now generally known as Buddha, to call upon the aboriginal races, and ultimately to convert the whole of Northern India to the religion that bears his name. It was not, however, till 300 years after his death, which happened in 543, that this faith became the religion of the state. This happened in the reign of king Asoka, about 250 years before Christ, and for 1000 years Buddhism continued the prevailing religion, though at the present

Façade of Cave in Behar (temp. Asoka, B.C. 250).

hour there is not a native-born Buddhist in India, and but for the monuments we might almost be allowed to doubt its prevalence.

It is with this religion, and this king Asoka, that our architectural history begins in India. Before his time we have nothing, and in the illustration we have a proof that then we ought not to expect to find anything. It is a well-authenticated example of his reign, and though cut in the granite rock, every form and every detail is copied from some wooden original, showing that at the time it was executed stone architecture was unknown in India, and men were only beginning to think of a more durable material. From that time we have hundreds of examples, in which we see the wooden forms gradually being replaced by those more appropriate to stone; and at last, after following it for 1000 years, we find it gradually fading into the style contemporaneously elaborated by the Jains and Hindus, and dying out with the religion that gave birth to it.

Leaving the valley of the Ganges, we find another great immigration taking place. This time it was that of the Dravidian tribes, but instead of Balkh and Bokhara, from which the Aryan tribes came, their seat was further south; they crossed the Lower Indus to Guzerat, but before we became acquainted with them they had got pressed down by subsequent immigrations into the southern angle of the peninsula. They now occupy the whole, or nearly so, of the Madras Presidency, and are one of the greatest building races in the world, but totally distinct from those found further north.

The next great immigration commenced a century or two before the Christian era, and continued through the centuries immediately following that event. They came across the Lower Indus, occupied Guzerat and Rajpootana, and eventually extended to the Mysore on the south, and to Agra and Delhi on the north. The fourth great immigration was that of the Mahommedans, from the 11th to the 13th and 14th centuries. They came across the Upper Indus, and eventually spread down as far as the Mysore, occupying the whole of India more nearly than any of the preceding races. The fifth civilization is our own. We are the only people who came, not across the Indus, but by sea; but, of course, I need not allude either to our ethnology or our art on the present occasion.

Whether it arises from the want of roads as means of communication, or from the absence of any great permanent capital or state, the great fact of Indian ethnography is that all these various people retain most of their individuality to the present day. What is, however, more to our present purpose is, that each and all of them have left most distinct traces of their peculiarities in the buildings they erected, and the different styles of architecture they from time to time adopted.

No one who travels through the country, and is familiar with such researches, can fail to perceive easily when and where the Buddhist religion arose, and how far it spread—how pure it was at first, and how it gradually became idolatrous and corrupt, and how at last it perished beneath its own overgrown hierarchy. Nor can he help seeing how and where the Jaina religion superseded Buddhism among the Rajpoots, and how that eventually degenerated into the religion of Vishnu, which is at present one of its most corrupted forms.

The limits of the Dravidian style are quite as strongly and clearly marked, and from this architecture we learn how far they ever penetrated northwards, and at what time, and from whence, and how they were pressed backwards by the northern races. We can also see the aboriginal tribes of Bengal, who were driven to the hills by the Aryans, and who retained their ancient faith in spite of the Buddhist reform, emerging again from their fastnesses in modern times, and gradually extending their style over the plains they had originally occupied. In fact, the architecture of the country may be considered as a great stone book, in which each tribe and race has written its annals and recorded its faith, and that in a manner so clear that those who run may read.

It may be objected that all this ethnography can be learned from the language of the people, and has already been done to a great extent. Perhaps it has; and, if you will learn Sanscrit and Pali, and all the Pracrits—if you will master Tamul and Teloogoo and Canarese—and study Bengalee, Maharattee, Gujerattee, and fifty other other dialects—and if you are tolerably familiar, in addition, with Persian and Turkish, you may acquire the knowledge I have been pointing out, provided you can ascertain where all or each of these languages is or was spoken in India, and when it was introduced or ceased to be used. Even then the architecture has the advantage, that it is more distinct, that it never shifts its locality, and that it does not change with time: and in India especially, where we have so many rock-cut examples, we know exactly what the religion, what the art, and what the

civilization of the people were who excavated them. We stand actually, as it were, beside the people who were hewing the mountain into form, and we can read the thoughts they then were wishing to express.

It is the same with the structural buildings. To take an instance among many. Here is a representation of temples at Badamee, on the limit between the northern and southern architectural provinces. Any one at all familiar with the subject will at once recognize the difference between the two.

That on the left is a straight-lined low pyramid, divided into storeys, and adorned with pilasters. That on the right is curvilinear, with no trace of storeys or pilasters, and instead of the domical form that crowns the one, it terminates in a conventional fruit-like ornament. I know that the people who erected the first must have been speaking Tamul or some of the allied languages when at work upon it, and that those who erected the other were speaking Bengalee or some tongue with a strong infusion of Sanscrit in its composition. If we knew their dates we could tell when the southern races extended so far north as this, or when the northern people penetrated so far south. So it is all over the country.

It seems almost impossible to over-estimate the value of these stone landmarks in a country where so few books exist, and so little history, and where what does exist is so very untrustworthy. So far as I can form an opinion, the architecture of India is not only the best means of elucidating the manners and customs of the country, but of checking their fables, and is frequently the only means that remain to us; and, if this be so, is it possible to over-estimate its value to those who wish to know who and what the people are or were, whom we have undertaken to guide and govern?

It is not, however, only the ethnography that the architecture of India seems so completely to illustrate. It equally seems to fix the ever-varying forms of the religion of that country, and to preserve them for our examination. In a country where printing was till very recently unknown, and where the climate is so destructive of writing materials, old books rarely exist, and it was too frequently the fashion to adapt each succeeding transcription to the taste and feeling of the day. It is, consequently, only by an appeal from the paper to the stone book, that we can know how far a religion had become degraded at any time, or when it prevailed, and by what people it is practised. One of the great characteristics of Indian Architecture is the profusion of sculpture, which forms an absolutely essential part of it. And in this sculpture, more truly than in any written document, we can read the exact form of faith at any particular period.

There is still another aspect in which the architecture is vitally important, and that is with regard to history. I need hardly tell you that in India there are no written annals which can be trusted. It is only when it can be authenticated by inscriptions and coins that we can feel sure of the existence of any King, and it is only when we can find his buildings that we can measure his greatness or ascertain what his tendencies were, or what the degree of civilization to which either he or his people had attained.

These are vast subjects, the extent of which can hardly be even indicated on the present occasion; but the point to which I especially wish to direct attention at present is this—if we take the period of Indian history which elapsed between Asoka, B.C. 250, and Mahmoud of Guzni, A.D. 1030, it is the darkest and most perplexed of the whole. There are no annals, properly so called—no authentic account of the religion, the manners and customs of the people, but throughout these thirteen centuries we have numerous buildings covered with sculpture, and frequently bearing inscriptions. They, and they only, tell us who the people were who occupied any particular locality, what their faith was at any particular period, and in what state of civilization and prosperity they then existed. If all this is engraved on the architecture of the country, I certainly feel justified in asserting that the study of it is worthy of the attention of all those who wish to know who the people of this great country are, and in what state they existed before the Mahommedan invasion first let the light of history into their annals. It is equally important to those who wish to know how far they have deteriorated and advanced under the rule of the Moslems; and still more, what effect our civilization has had on the natives of India.

PART II.

Before attempting to explain to you the importance of Indian Architecture as bearing on our own, allow me to guard myself most distinctly against anything I am about to say being construed into a recommendation to copy any of the forms or details of the Indian styles. My conviction is, that the system of copying different styles is the great—if not the sole cause of the present anomalous style of the art, and if I thought anything I said would encourage such a practice I would be silent. Although, therefore, I must consider copying the Indian styles as a crime, I feel convinced that there are principles underlying them which cannot be too deeply studied, and that there are many suggestions to be derived from the practice of the Indian architect which cannot fail, if properly used, to be useful to our own. The great merit, however, of the study I conceive to be the widening of our base of observation, and so enabling students to realise the true definition of the art, for till that is grasped there seems little hope of any improvement in our architecture.

I may perhaps make what I mean clearer by referring to our own recent experience. During the last century, when the education of gentlemen was confined to the classics, we knew and practised only Roman architecture; and as the middle and lower orders of our countrymen had no sympathy with Doric or Corinthian orders, they were content to go without architecture altogether. In the beginning of the century, Greek architecture was practically discovered, and eagerly adopted by the highly-educated classes, but in the same manner as the other. We copied it without having any real sympathy with it. At last we discovered that the Middle Ages had also an architecture of their own, and one with which we had, or might have, infinitely more sympathy. This was an enormous gain, not only because it enlisted a much wider class in the art, but more—because it taught the architects how much wider the field of architectural design was, than had been originally supposed. Unfortunately, we took to copying Gothic art, as we then copied Classical, and so far retarded progress. At last we begin to be tired of reproducing old things, and are beginning to think, instead of copying. The first symptom of this is, that classical designs are not so rigidly classical as they were, but a certain amount of Gothic feeling is instilled into them; and Gothic designs are sometimes not so ludicrously mediæval as they used to be, but a certain amount of refinement and of modern feeling and adaptation is thought expedient in civil, though hardly yet in ecclesiastical, architecture. The two are approaching one another. When they are fused, we shall have an architecture of our own; and I know nothing so likely to lead to such a result, as the study of an entirely foreign style like that of India. I feel certain that no one can familiarise himself with Indian art without feeling that the architects of that country were as successful as either those of Rome or the Middle Ages, in reaching the aims they were aspiring to; though, in doing this, they employed arrangements as different as possible from those we are furnished with, and adopted details and forms diametrically opposed in principle to those we have hitherto been taught to admire. Of course a man requires to familiarise himself with these forms before he can admire them, and he must understand their application before he can appreciate their adaptability; but once he has conquered this, it seems to me impossible he should arrive at any other conclusion than this:—That there is no form into which stone can be carved which is not beautiful, if it is appropriate to the purpose for which it is employed; and that no one form is preferable in architecture to any other form, except in so far as it is better adapted constructively for the situation in which it is employed, or artistically more aptly expresses the purpose of the building of which it forms a part.

The principle, in fact, is the same that pervades all the works of nature. I defy any one to give a good logical reason why the form of a man's nose, or ear, or head, is beautiful. There is nothing in the shape of an eye, or an arm, or leg, or hand, or foot, that is beautiful abstractively; but they are all beautiful, because they are exquisitely adapted to the purposes to which they are applied. So in every animal and every plant; when we understand and appreciate its structure, we see beauty in all its forms. It is the highest merit of the art of architecture, that of all man's works, it is that which most closely copies the principles which we gather from a study of the works of nature. Its greatest glory is, that in architecture man adapts means to an end, and employs ornament in exactly the same manner—in so far as we can understand it—as nature follows in the creation of plants and animals. It is a creative, not a copying art, and, though in an immensely lower degree, it is creative exactly in the same sense in which all understand the creative powers of nature, and may be judged of and criticised by the same rules.

As architecture has hitherto been studied, it has been impossible to perceive this; and so long as we continue cribbed in the narrow school of Classical or Gothic art, it will be impossible to rise to such considerations. Once a man gets out of that groove, and perceives how wide the field is, and how certain the result when following certain principles of common sense, the art becomes easy and failure impossible, and that principle may, I conceive, be more easily learnt in India than anywhere else I know of. This facility of learning arises not only from the immense number and variety of the ancient examples in every part of that country, but because you may at the present day see those who can neither read, nor write, nor draw, building temples and palaces as beautiful in form and detail as those of their forefathers, and which are not copies, but elaborated on the same principles as resulted in the productions of our great mediæval cathedrals. But I must not detain you too long with these abstract doctrines. The lesson, I conceive, that every one must learn who studies such an art as that of India is, that a man can hardly fail in producing a good design if he thinks only of what he is doing, and how he can do it best. Not only in architecture, but in every similar art, a thoroughly purpose-like and appropriate design must be permanently successful. The most obvious proof of this is that in Egypt, as in Greece and Rome; in the Middle Ages, in India and Cambodia, or China; even in Mexico and Peru; in every age and in every part of the world, men, in every stage of civilization, succeeded in producing beautiful and appropriate objects of architecture. Failure was unknown, till in the fifteenth century some evil-disposed persons took it into their heads to revive, by copying classical art. Since that day success has been impossible, notwithstanding all our civilization and power, and all our mechanical skill; for since then nothing but failure after failure has marked the architecture of Europe. If, however, an architect could once be taught to think, independently of copying, I feel convinced they might easily surpass all that has hitherto been done; and I do not know how they could learn this so easily and so pleasantly, as by the study of an art which differs from all they have hitherto been accustomed to admire, but which still attains its ends as certainly and as successfully, as was done in any of those styles with which we have up to this time been familiar.

Turning from these principles to the suggestions that may be derived from the study of Indian art, we approach a subject that admits of infinite illustration. I must, however, confine myself only to such as will explain what I mean, without attempting to do more. One of the best illustrations for the purpose that occurs to me, is that of the arrangement of Jaina domes. Every one will, I fancy, admit that abstractedly the dome is the most beautiful form of roof that has yet been invented, but there are very great difficulties in fitting its circular outline to the square and rectangular form of our halls and churches, and it is in consequence rarely employed in Europe.

In India they have surmounted these difficulties with great success, and generally in the following manner. As a rule the dome rests on eight pillars; but as an octagonal outline is necessarily a weak one, they almost invariably add four pillars, one on each angle, which makes up the number to 12, and the figure to a square. This in itself forms a very pleasing pavilion, and this form is very generally used. When an extension is wanted, two pillars are added on each face, making a quasi-cruciform plan, with 20 pillars; or again, 4 are added on each face, making 36 pillars; or again, 5 on each face, making

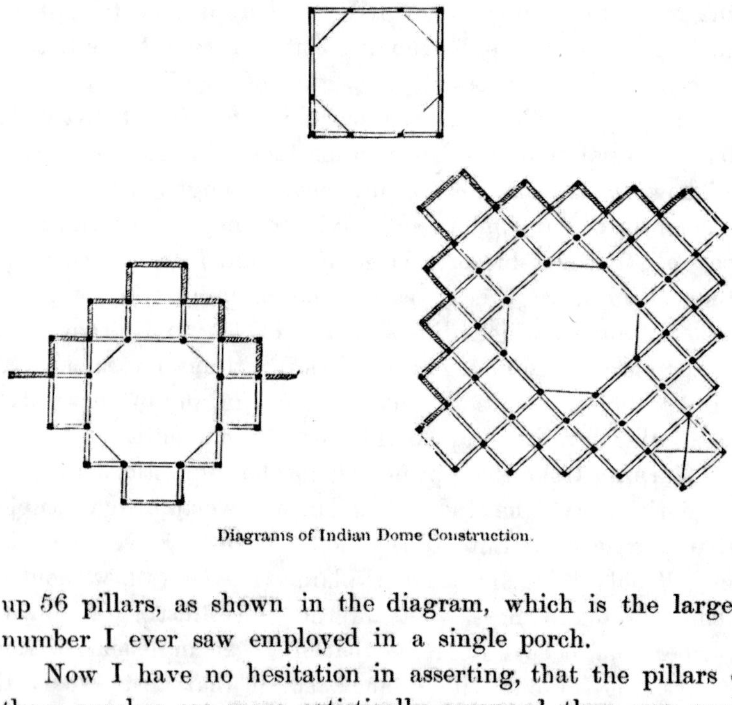

Diagrams of Indian Dome Construction.

up 56 pillars, as shown in the diagram, which is the largest number I ever saw employed in a single porch.

Now I have no hesitation in asserting, that the pillars of these porches are more artistically arranged than any equal number in any building in the West. In the first place, the octagon in the centre has the happy property, that when its sides are produced into a square they are in the ratio of 10 to 7, and this proportion consequently pervades the whole structure, the length of the greater and lesser aisles being in the same ratio. In Gothic buildings, the ratio of the side to the centre aisles is as one to two generally, and the height of the principal one is also doubled. In India they are of one height, and just in that proportion which is best suited to give dignity to the central without overpowering the side aisles. By this arrangement, also, the principal aisles are longer than the minor ones in the same ratio, as they run along the diagram of the square. But the greatest beauty of the arrangement, perhaps, is the position of the dome in the centre, exactly where dignity is wanted. The only attempt at a similar effect in Gothic Architecture is at Ely. The central lantern there is beautiful in so far as it follows these arrangements, and fails just when it ceases to carry them to their legitimate extent.

Externally, the effect is as happy as it is internally. The breaking up of the external parts gives a play of light and shade, and a sparkling brilliancy of effect, not to be obtained by any other process that I am aware of; the salient and re-entering angles give those vertical lines which the Gothic architects sought, somewhat clumsily, to attain by the employment of buttresses and other mechanical expedients, and the classic architects still more clumsily, by the employment of pilasters and three-quarter columns. The Hindoos alone seem to have effected this by true constructive expedients.

Fortunately, any one who wishes to form an opinion as to the beauty of this arrangement internally, can do so by paying a visit to the Church of St. Stephen's, Walbrook. It is avowedly Sir Christopher Wren's masterpiece, and, both on the Continent and in this country, allowed to be one of the most beautiful classical interiors erected in modern times. The success is entirely owing to its architect having hit upon the same idea as the Jaina dome builders. In some respects it is inferior to them, but this arises either from the space in the City being limited, or Sir Christopher Wren not having carried the principle far enough.

It is not only, however, in constructive arrangement that

the Indian architects might afford important suggestions. There are probably few things our Gothic antiquarians are so justly proud of as our window tracery; but I question if there is anything in Europe of that class so beautiful as the windows of the Bhudder at Ahmedabad. There is just that admixture of constructive forms with those of conventionalised nature, which makes up the perfection of decoration in all styles; and if those windows were glazed with coloured mosaic glass, with that brilliant harmony so general in the East, it would be difficult to match them for beauty in their class, from examples in any other style.

Window of the Bhudder at Ahmedabad.

Besides these, however, there are some hundreds of examples of the same class of decoration at Ahmedabad used merely as ornament, and, consequently, hardly constructive, but such as might be freely imitated in metal or in terra-cotta, and if used appropriately, would be more beautiful than anything of the kind we have yet seen.

One other peculiarity of our Gothic style, to which we are accustomed to turn with pride, is the form of the pendants from our Gothic roofs. Those, however, which the Jains in Guzerat hung from the centre of their domes, are not only more beautiful in form, but far richer in ornament, and every detail so exquisitely designed to the place in which it is put, that our Gothic architect must yield the palm to them, as in this or in other respects.

It would be easy to go on multiplying examples of this sort, but time will not permit, and without detailed illustration it is impossible to make the subject understood, and I shall not therefore attempt it. Before concluding, however, let me call your attention to another subject, though its interest is more archæological than artistic. You have all heard what a bone of contention the age of cromlechs, dolmens, and menhirs are to our antiquaries, and how much divine wrath the subject excites in certain bosoms. Now here is a new fact for discussion. In the spring of the present year a surveyor—luckily not a railway surveyor, for had it been the latter the monuments would before this have been utilized, but one employed in the trigonometrical survey—in cutting his way through the Neermull jungle, half-way between Hydrabad and Nagpore, came to a group of cromlechs and crosses, of which he made some photographs, and sent them home. The cromlechs are identical in every form with those in Brittany and Wales. The crosses, nine to ten feet in height, are such as might be found in Ireland or in Kensal Green Cemetery. That they are of Christian origin can hardly be doubted, and that they are of the same age as the cromlechs seems a certainty, and that the two forms belonged to the same people. Who those people were, and when they lived, I must leave to others to determine. All I wish to point out here is, that it is another point of interest in the study of architecture in India.

Allow me, before concluding, to recapitulate as briefly but as clearly as I can, the principal points on which I have dwelt in the preceding paper, in order that you may judge how far I have made out my case, or made myself understood.

I consider the study of Indian Architecture important, because it affords the readiest and most direct means of ascertaining the ethnological relations of the different races inhabiting India. It points out more clearly than can be done by other means, how they succeeded each other, where they settled, how they mixed, or when they were absorbed.

In the next place, I consider it important, because it affords the best picture of the religious faiths of the country, showing how and when they arose, how they became corrupted, and when and by what steps they sank to their present level.

It is also, I believe, important, because in a country which has no written histories, it affords almost the only means that exist for steadying any conclusion we may arrive at, and is a measure of the greatness or decay of the dynasties that ruled that country in ancient times.

These considerations refer wholly to India, and to the importance of the study as bearing on Indian questions only; but I consider it as important also, because of its bearings on architectural art in our own country. First, because by widening the base of our observations and extending our views to a style wholly different from our own, we are able to look at architecture from a new and outside point of view, and by doing this, to master principles which are wholly hidden from those whose study is confined to one style so mixed up with adventitious associations as our local styles inevitably are.

It also is important, because architecture in India is still a living art. We can see there, at the present day, buildings as important as works of art, as our mediæval cathedrals erected by master masons, on precisely the same principle and in the same manner that guided our mediæval masons to such glorious results.

It also is, I conceive, important, as offering many suggestions, which, if adopted in a modified form, might tend considerably to the improvement of our own architectural designs.

Lastly, I consider the study worthy of attention from the light it may be expected to throw on some of our own archæological problems.

Besides these seven, there are many other reasons that I could urge, to prove that the study is worthy of more attention than it has hitherto received; but if I have succeeded in making these at all clear, they are amply sufficient to my purpose. If you feel at all with me on the subject, I need no apology for concluding by saying that if Indian Architecture is worthy of study, it is worth while that something should be done to obtain the materials requisite for that purpose; and I do hope that some sort of organization may be got together to collect and bring home such representations of Indian buildings as may render the study easy and accessible to all. A good deal has been done lately, but it has been done without system. Those temples only have been photographed which are situated near where some artist with the necessary apparatus happened to reside. Many of the most important are still unrepresented. In no instance—except one—have they been accompanied with the plans or measurements or descriptions necessary to make them intelligible, without at least a very disproportionate amount of study. By organization all these difficulties might be avoided, and with it I think the results would be such as would surpass the most sanguine anticipations.

If anything is to be done, it ought to be done quickly, for in a tropical country like that of India, 'Decay's effacing fingers' work much more rapidly than in a temperate climate. Vegetation there is also an active power, always tending to tear down temples and destroy the most elaborate buildings; and there is a third power more perniciously active than either in the shape of the barrack department, which is fast obliterating beauty in the land. Within the last few years, one-half of the palace at Delhi has been pulled down to make way for a regimental barrack. The fort of Gwalior has still more recently been handed over to the department, and everywhere, from the causes above-mentioned, destruction is stalking over the land; and unless something is done, and done quickly, to perpetuate by representation the forms of those beautiful buildings, it may be too late, and their memory pass away for ever.

DISCUSSION.

Mr. Henry Cole, C.B., remarked, that if anything were wanting to convince Englishmen how much there was in India of which they were ignorant, it was the able paper they had heard this evening. His own impression was, that they knew very little indeed of India, excepting what they read in prices current of grey shirtings, twills, cotton twist, indigo, and the like. Of the people of India they knew very little; and of their architecture still less. He thought it hardly too much to say that there were scarcely half-a-dozen architects in this country who could pass an examination in Indian architecture; and yet here was the great fact that there was an architecture, whether beautiful or ugly did not affect the question, which might be said to give the history of a people living in a state of considerable civilization even 500 years before the Christian era. That the architects of this country should know very little about Indian architecture was not surprising, when it was recollected that even within the memory of members not older than himself, they knew very little about Gothic architecture. Fifty years ago, nobody knew anything about Gothic architecture, and he remembered being sent to look at the new church of St. Luke's, Chelsea, as something wonderful and novel. We knew how great a revival there had been in that branch of art. If such had been the case with Gothic architecture, he thought that eventually they might hope to have some little knowledge, at least, of the architecture of India. Not more than a hundred years ago, Horace Walpole built that structure, which was then thought to be excellent Gothic, at Strawberry Hill; and scarcely fifty years had elapsed since Wyatt, in Durham Cathedral, and elsewhere, exercised his taste in what he considered to be Gothic; and yet at the present time, there was not an architect's pupil who would not consider himself disgraced if he had produced such works. He therefore did not despair of seeing Indian architecture studied in this country. He did not desire to see it copied. As to the suggestions it offered, he might mention that visitors to Paris next year would see a building in connexion with the Exhibition there, the design of which was somewhat in the form of an Indian temple photographed in Mr. Hope's book on architecture. In the English department of the Paris Exhibition it had been found necessary to erect a building to contain several boilers, which were in the first place to be exhibited as specimens of manufacture, and also to be used to drive the machinery. Of course, in connexion with the boilers there must be a chimney, and it was desired to have it ornamental; the building must also be extremely airy, so as to make it as cool as possible. Looking over Mr. Hope's work on architecture, was found a representation of a mosque of which Syud Oosman was said

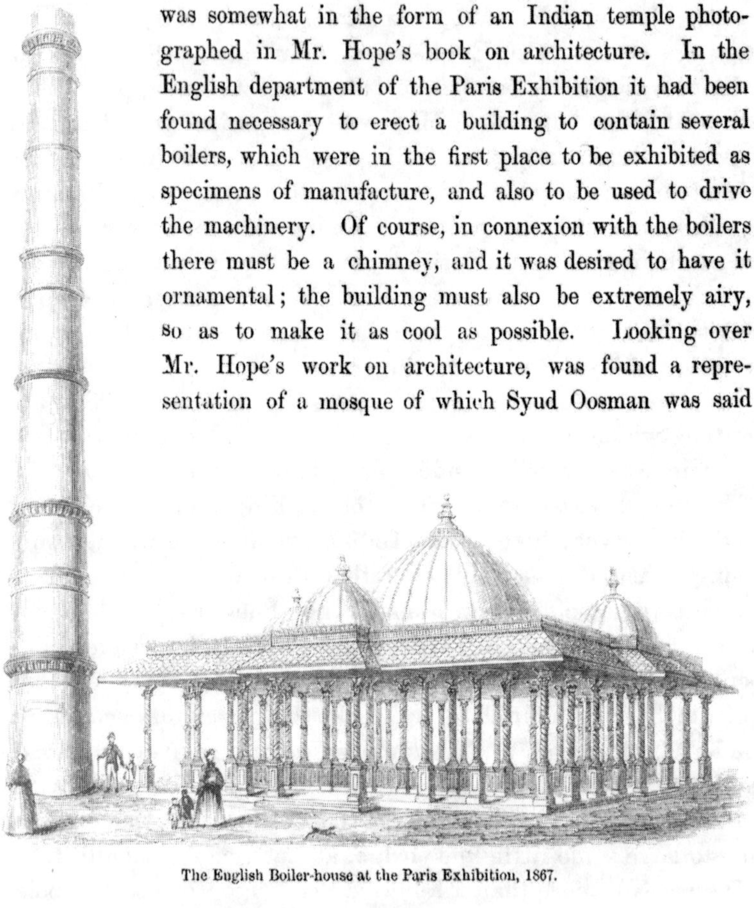

The English Boiler-house at the Paris Exhibition, 1867.

to have been the builder, and this gave, in addition to extremely ornamental forms like chimneys, colonnades which afforded open spaces for the public to inspect the boilers in. It afforded suggestions for the exact building wanted. It was most remarkable how much influence the display of Indian productions shown in the Exhibition of

1851 had had upon our taste, especially in the manufacture of carpets and other fabrics. Mr. Peter Graham, a competent witness, was present, and could testify to this. Instead of flaring patterns in perspective, they had decorous flat patterns, on which they could place furniture without feelings of discomfort, and it was the fact that a large trade had since been established in Masulipatam carpets. The same influence, he believed, would ultimately be exerted by the architecture as by the manufactures of India. He also remembered that in the Exhibition of 1851, whilst they had these beautiful patterns designed by the "benighted" people of India, there were beside them some most abominable imitations of European patterns from India. Indeed, there was nothing so bad as when an Indian attempted to imitate European art; and he confessed he had some fear lest the Schools of Design lately established in Calcutta, Madras, and Bombay, instead of leading the natives to advance in their own styles of art, should create a hybrid style, the most detestable ever seen. In his opinion, we had a great deal more to learn from the Indians than we could hope to teach them in the designing of patterns, and he protested against Schools of Art in India, which should corrupt native talent and taste. He might mention another point. He read in the *Builder* a little time ago, that for the University of Calcutta it had been determined to adopt the Doric style of architecture. It might possibly be right to have Doric columns in the University of Calcutta, but it could hardly be right that they should be of cast stucco imported from England. Could they conceive anything more likely to debase Indian art than taking cast stucco columns from England to Calcutta? Mr. Fergusson had alluded to the importance of having some kind of systematic mode of collecting information on the architecture of India. He was quite sure, supposing they none of them cared at all about art, they must nevertheless feel an interest in the millions of human beings, who were at present subjects of Queen Victoria, and must long to know something about these remarkable people. He would ask how that rude cross and cromlech, shown in a diagram on the walls, could have got into the place where it was described to have been found? It was a veritable duplicate of Kit's Cotty-house in Kent, and yet it was in the midst of a dense jungle. Let them try and penetrate the history of such things as these. Mr. Fergusson had suggested that they should go on systematically obtaining photographic representations of objects of art in India. He (Mr. Cole) hoped some plan would be arranged by which we might be able to have in this country a systematic collection of photographs of Indian buildings; there were already skilful photographers high up in the hills in India, who were in possession of thousands of these photographs, and he hoped we should soon see them in this country. He was enabled to state that it was intended that in the Indian court of the Paris Exhibition, Indian architecture should be represented. In addition to photographs, he would suggest plans, sections, and casts. Only the difficulty of cost, which Englishmen very soon overcame, stood in the way of procuring casts of all the typical buildings of India. The public money had been already employed in obtaining casts of the finest objects in Italy, Spain, and France. We had recently imported into this country, at a cost of between 2000*l.* and 3000*l.*, a cast of the beautiful gate of the convent of Santiago, in Spain; and if it were well to have these casts from Spain, it would be well to have them from India also. This was the more important when it was recollected how rapid was the destruction of such works in that country from various causes; and while on this subject, he would read the following extract from a work on the architecture of Ahmedabad, which showed how wantonly even those who ought to respect such monuments sometimes treated them:—

"Sedee Syeed's mosque at Ahmedabad is now built into the north-eastern corner of the modern wall of the 'Bhudder.' Its position exposed it in after times to more than usually rough treatment. After being desecrated by the Mahrattas, it has been converted by the British into one of the public offices, and has been hacked about to suit official convenience as much as the Chapter House at Westminster. But its principal glory still remains intact in two windows of perforated marble, which may be safely affirmed to be unrivalled throughout the East. Their dimensions are ten feet wide by seven feet high."—*Architecture of A'medabad*, pp. 46, 47. (See illustration p. 20.)

Though he sympathised with the feelings that would abstain from robbing a country of its treasures, yet he thought when they were converting palaces and mosques into barracks and offices for Government clerks, they might be allowed to put in a word on behalf of saving treasures like those described by Mr. Fergusson, and applying them to more appropriate uses.* If the India Museum to be in Downing Street could not be adequately extended, some other place might be found in which those rich stores of ancient art might be deposited. Members would recollect, that in 1852 this Society announced its intention of forming a large and comprehensive exhibition of Indian art. A correspondence on the subject was opened with the Indian authorities, and their late President, the Prince Consort, was consulted, and gave his cordial support to the plan. Various difficulties, however, prevented the realization of the scheme, and the objects already collected were handed over to the authorities of the Dublin Exhibition. If the Society would, at a future time, again take up the idea, and hold a complete Indian Exhibition, embracing a proper representation of architecture, coupled, perhaps, with a complete Colonial exhibition, he believed a most interesting and valuable display would result. Speaking as a member of the Society and not as one of the Council, he would urge upon the members, if they took an inte-

---

* Major Alexander Cunningham of the Bengal Engineers in 1854 recommended that the two fallen gateways of the Sanchi Tope should be removed to the British Museum, which would ensure their preservation.

He also expressed a hope that the Court of Directors would cause the numerous Topes which still exist in North and South Bahar to be opened, and a report to be made on all the Buddhist remains of Kapila and Kusimrgara, of Vaisala and Rajagriha, which were the principal scenes of Sakya's labours.

rest in the subject, to endeavour to get up a thorough representation of the arts and manufactures of India, as well as of the products and raw materials of its commerce. On the occasion to which he had alluded, in the year 1852, there was great difficulty in providing a building for the exhibition, but that difficulty would in a year or two be removed. There would then be in existence a building, the great Central Hall, which would be sufficiently large to accommodate an exhibition of this kind, besides a good many other things.

Colonel Scott, R.E., would take the opportunity of asking Mr. Fergusson to what extent he considered the architecture of any one of these races of India had influenced the architecture of the race that succeeded it, and whether in the architecture of the present day any purer system was followed, or whether what was styled by Mr. Cole a hybrid character of architecture now prevailed in India?

Mr. Fergusson replied,—The styles in India had changed like those in this country, but each was a complete indication of the race of people to which it belonged. Each style differed from the preceding one, but was entirely without foreign admixture; and when they were familiar with the whole, the ethnology of the people was distinctly to be traced in the different styles. Where European influences prevailed architecturally, as in Lucknow and Hyderabad, the style had become corrupt and bad to the last degree, and all Mr. Cole had said was not half the truth.

Mr. J. Crawfurd said the architecture of India was certainly wonderful and curious, though he thought not very beautiful or graceful; and he contended that we were a more advanced people in this respect than those of India.

Mr. Peter Graham observed, that Mr. Cole having appealed

to him with regard to the influence exerted upon the manufactures of this country by the Indian department of the Exhibition of 1851, he had no hesitation in stating he entirely concurred in the views of that gentleman. He believed he was warranted in saying, that in the choicest specimen of ornamentation of the *cinque-cento* period, there might be traced an influence derived from Eastern objects of art that had been seen by the artists of that period. This could be discerned most distinctly; and he thought they could not do better than study those works — he did not mean as copyists — but as affording suggestions by which taste in the manufactures of this country might be improved.

Mr. Robert Rawlinson, C.B., considered that the employing architects and engineers, and allowing them to send out articles from this country for use in India, was an enormous waste of the public money. He knew that many things sent out from this country to India served no better purpose than affording a good commission to the parties who gave the orders for them. In water-works construction, it was evident that the Hindoos were in advance of us. There were reservoirs in India 2000 years old, and we might learn a lesson from them in this respect.

Mr. J. Beavington Atkinson believed the earliest building of which they had a record was something like 250 years before Christ, whereas Thebes and Memphis were supposed to have been founded 2000 years before Christ, and Rome 750 years; whilst the great period of the Greeks was, he believed, nearly contemporaneous with some of the photographs exhibited. Therefore, he would ask Mr. Fergusson how much further it was possible to go back in chronology, in order to arrive at the ethnography of the arts of India, and whether between the Eastern and Western architectures there could be traced any correspondence as to the details?

Mr. Philip Palmer answered some remarks of Mr. Rawlinson.

Mr. Fergusson, in reply upon the discussion, said Mr. Rawlinson laboured under a mistake in the views he had expressed relative to the square form of temple he referred to. It was impossible within the limits of a paper to point out all the details, but there were no separate apartments in the building, as Mr. Rawlinson had supposed; but the building, of which the plan was given on p. 26, was, in fact, a vast porch, standing on 56 pillars, and was perfectly open, the ventilation being, of course, in excess. The Dravidian temple belonged to a different style of architecture and a different age altogether. He had endeavoured to make it clear that he by no means wished these productions to be copied. All he said was, that there were principles in these buildings which were worthy of the study of architects, and it was by going to foreign styles, where they were not hampered by association, that they could most clearly understand what the true principles of architecture were. With regard to the remarks of Mr. Crawfurd, as to the absence of domestic architecture in India, that gentleman must surely be aware of the existence of numerous large and beautiful palaces, which, in point of form and ornamentation, were equal to anything in Europe. In reply to the question of Mr. Atkinson, as to how far Mahommedan architecture was Hindoo, and why he had applied the term Mahommedan to it, he would refer to the circumstance that when the Mahommedans went to Constantinople they did not take with them the architecture of Cairo, Syria, Spain, or Persia, but they literally copied the church of St. Sophia, which they found there, in the works which they erected in that city. Wherever the Mahommedans went they introduced no style of their own, but employed the native people to build their mosques for them; and this accounted for the fact that some of the most beautiful Mahommedan buildings in India were purely Hindoo from first to last. With regard to the ethnography of the buildings, he could not in India get beyond 250 years before Christ, but, as far as general knowledge on the subject went, from the building of the first pyramid in Egypt down to the present day in India, and down to the fifteenth century in Europe, there was not a single building which did not more or less mark the ethnography of the people who built it. What gave the study of architecture the greatest interest, was the fact that they could trace this ethnological relation not only in India, but also in Africa and China, and other parts of the world. Indian architecture itself formed but a small branch of this subject, though a pleasing and important one, because, from the want of inter-communication, they retained their peculiar idiosyncracies to a larger extent and more distinctly than any other people he knew. With regard to the request made by Mr. Graham, he should be happy that the photographs should go to South Kensington; but he hoped before long there would be a better collection in that establishment.

Sir Thomas Phillips, Q.C., said, before the closing of the discussion on the admirable paper they had heard, it might not be inappropriate to the presence of the Chairman (Sir James Fergusson), that the meeting should pronounce what he was sure they all felt, viz. that it was the duty of the Government of this country to do what in them lay to preserve as far as possible the recollection of those great architectural works throughout our Indian dependencies. Without entering into the disputed question of how far those buildings were really beautiful, there seemed no doubt that, as the rulers of a great people, who had occupied a territory extending over a considerable part of the globe, for a period of 2000 or 3000 years, it was the duty of the British Government to preserve, as far as might be, the memory of those great and distinctive works of art. Happily, we were in possession of an art which enabled us to preserve the representation of these great monuments at small cost and with great accuracy; and he could not doubt that means would be taken for obtaining, especially by means of photography, such memorials as might be regarded as objects of real national interest.

The Chairman said the evident interest with which the meeting had listened to the very valuable paper which Mr. Fergusson had delivered, made him feel that it would be a mere matter of form on his part to propose that the meeting should accord their most grateful thanks to that gentleman. But he could not omit the opportunity to say how greatly the gratification he had felt at the honour conferred upon him, in being invited to occupy this distinguished chair, had been enhanced by the deep interest he had felt in listening to Mr. Fergusson's paper. It was certainly an unusual thing for an Under-Secretary of State for India to vary his ordinary duties, which he hoped were not altogether useless, by attending such a meeting as this, and hearing such a subject discussed. He was usually confined to the drier matters of how to make Indian railways pay; how to pay the public servants in India; and too often, perhaps, how not to pay them. In some of the speeches delivered this evening, rather pointed allusions had been made to the responsibilities of the Home Government of India, in which he had the honour to hold a humble position; and some slight imputation was cast upon the Government on account of what were considered breaches of taste in connexion with public works in India. It should, however, be remembered, that the government of India was mainly conducted in that country; and not only were the public works promoted there, but the duty of preserving the ancient monuments of the country must be discharged by those who were on the spot. Great as the influence of this Society was, there were kindred societies in India, which showed that Europeans in that country were not unmindful of the subject which had been treated this evening; and the Society at home might be doing wrong in taking the matter out of their hands, inasmuch as through their agency, working through the government of India, they might accomplish the end in view. Undoubtedly, it was desirable to possess authentic records of these monuments of ancient times, but it might be a question with those who had to administer the scanty revenues of India, as to how far the public funds should be devoted to such a purpose. He ventured to think, that if they wished to obtain these records from India, it could only be done for the most part by private enterprise; at the same time, he was quite sure that the men at the head of the government were far too enlightened to be unmindful of these works of art, and that they would only be too happy to facilitate opportunities for procuring the memorials referred to, for any benefit thus conferred upon the arts in this country would be reflected back upon the people of India themselves. He believed the more the people of this country—especially the educated and learned classes—were led to bend their thoughts towards that great dependency, which involved such deep responsibilities upon ourselves, the greater would be the amount of benefit to the people of India; and he hoped that indirectly this might be the means of attracting more of the capital of this country to the development of the commercial resources of India, while at the same time our rule there was not unmarked by attention to those arts which refined and civilised mankind. He was sure he carried with him the feeling of the meeting, in tendering to Mr. Fergusson their cordial thanks for the paper he had favoured them with.

The vote of thanks was passed unanimously.